Riddles & Trivia Questions

for Smart Kids

A Fun Family Book Filled with
Conversation Starters and Challenges -
Great for Kids, Teens and Adults

Contents

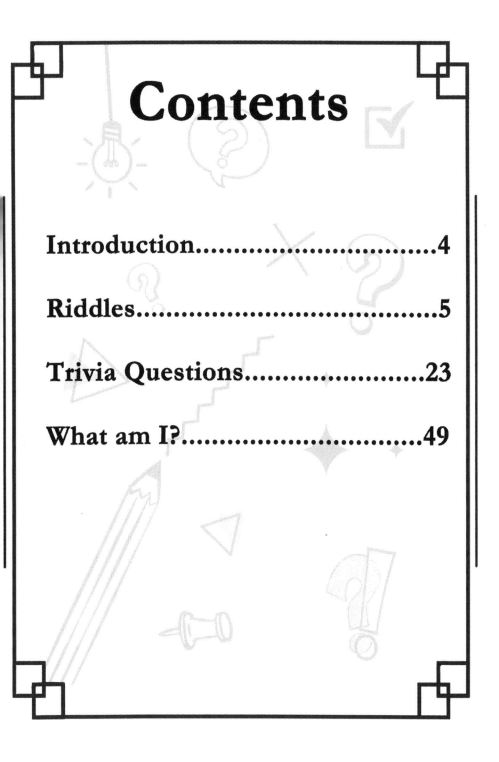

Introduction

If you're looking for a new and exciting family activity, then keep reading!

Who doesn't love riddles and trivia?
Make your family nights and weekends come alive with a new family activity that everyone will love with "Riddles and Trivia Questions for smart kids"!
Creating fond family memories while learning exciting conversation starters and doing challenges is always welcome in anyone's house.
Get in on the fun and enjoy a fun new way to bond with everyone — even when you're all stuck at home!

In this fun family book, you will enjoy:
- Fun riddles that tickle everyone's imaginations
- Trivia questions that can make even the family geniuses pause and think
- What am I? Riddles that can kick start the fun in no time and any day.

Grab a few of your friends or family members, and give the gift of fun to anyone who loves trivia and riddles so they, too, can keep the party going all day, every day!

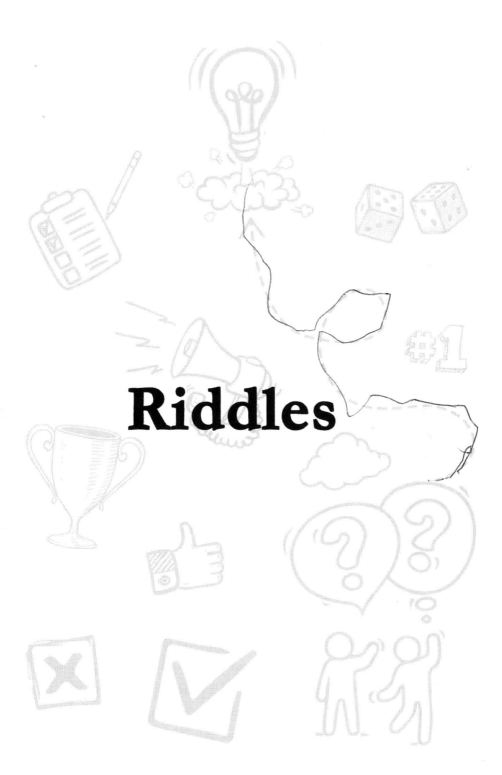

Riddles

Fun Riddles

Q. During which month do people sleep the least?

A. February

Q. What kind of room has no doors or windows?

A. A mushroom

Fun Riddles

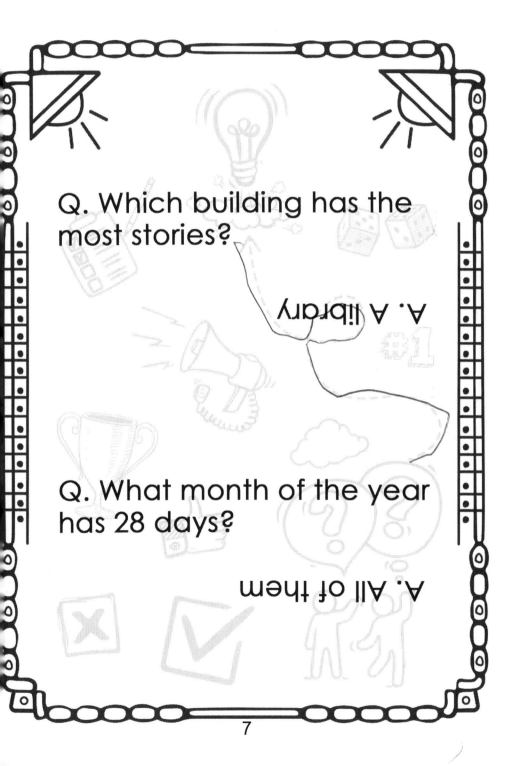

Q. Which building has the most stories?

A. A library

Q. What month of the year has 28 days?

A. All of them

Fun Riddles

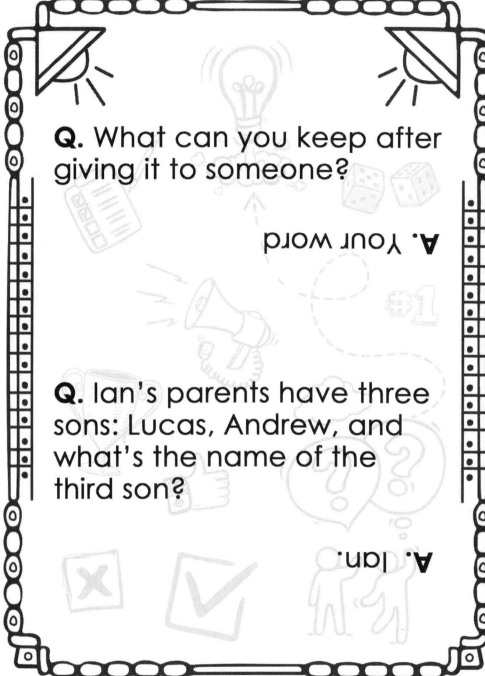

Q. What can you keep after giving it to someone?

A. Your word

Q. Ian's parents have three sons: Lucas, Andrew, and what's the name of the third son?

A. Ian.

Fun Riddles

Q. What has a neck but no head?

A. A bottle

Q. What has many needles, but doesn't sew?

A. A Christmas tree

Fun Riddles

Q. What has words, but never speaks?

A. A book

Q. What do you find at the end of a rainbow?

A. The letter W

Fun Riddles

Q. What 2 things can you never eat for breakfast?

A. Lunch and dinner

Q. Two fathers and two sons are in a car, yet there are only three people in the car. How?

A. They are a grandfather, father and son

Fun Riddles

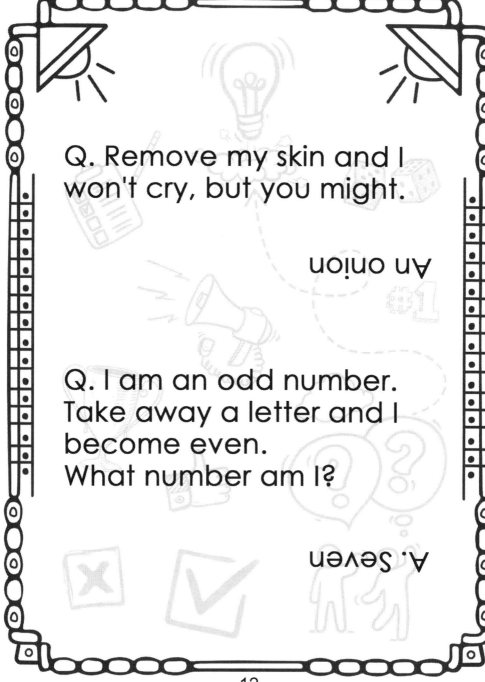

Q. Remove my skin and I won't cry, but you might.

A. An onion

Q. I am an odd number. Take away a letter and I become even. What number am I?

A. Seven

Fun Riddles

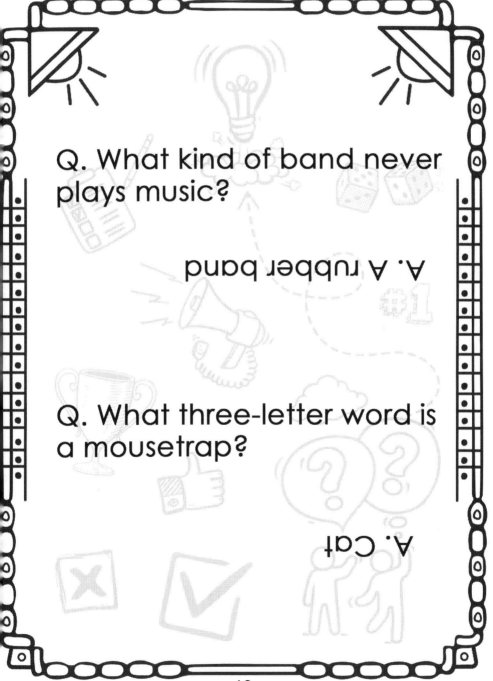

Q. What kind of band never plays music?

A. A rubber band

Q. What three-letter word is a mousetrap?

A. Cat

Fun Riddles

Q. What bus crossed the ocean?

A. Columbus

Q. What did one wall say to another?

A. Meet you at the corner

Fun Riddles

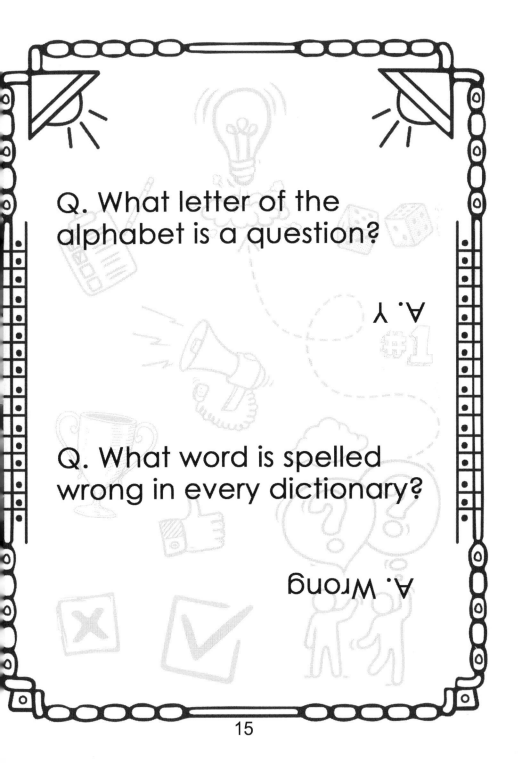

Q. What letter of the alphabet is a question?

A. Y

Q. What word is spelled wrong in every dictionary?

A. Wrong

Fun Riddles

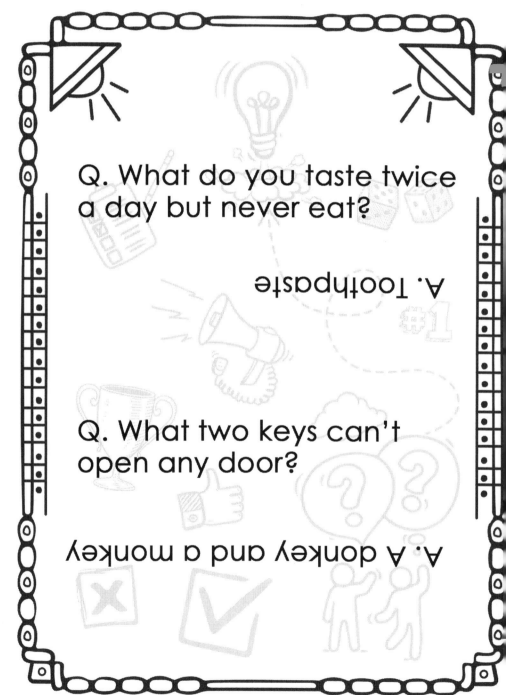

Q. What do you taste twice a day but never eat?

A. Toothpaste

Q. What two keys can't open any door?

A. A donkey and a monkey

Fun Riddles

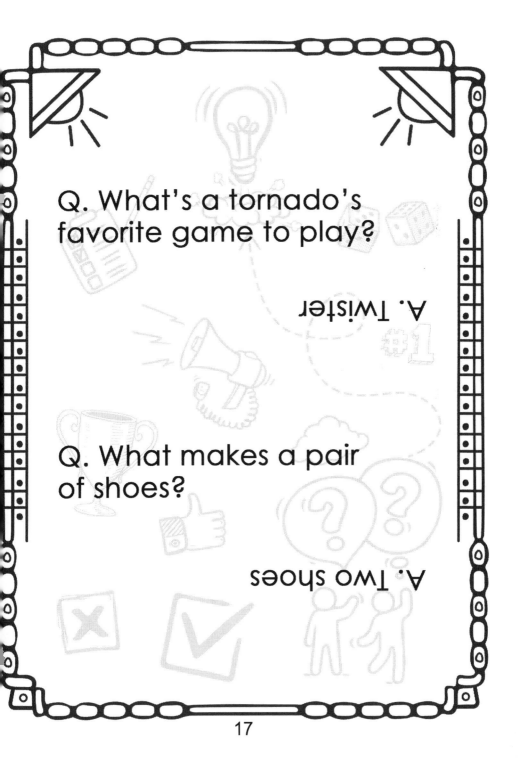

Q. What's a tornado's favorite game to play?

A. Twister

Q. What makes a pair of shoes?

A. Two shoes

Fun Riddles

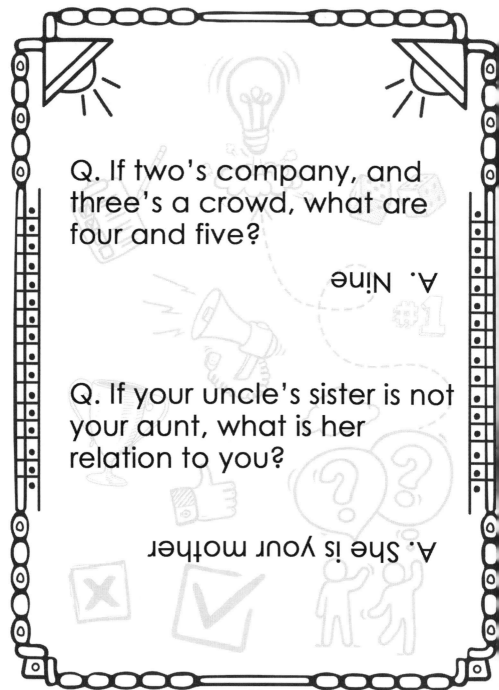

Q. If two's company, and three's a crowd, what are four and five?

A. Nine

Q. If your uncle's sister is not your aunt, what is her relation to you?

A. She is your mother

Fun Riddles

Q. What would you find in the middle of Toronto?

A. The letter O

Q. If there are three apples and you take away two, how many apples do you have?

A. You have two apples

Fun Riddles

Q. What is the best and cheapest light?

A. Daylight

Q. What breaks yet never falls, and what falls yet never breaks?

A. Day and night

Trivia Questions
&
Answers

Trivia Questions & Answers

Q. What contains more sugar: strawberries or lemons?
A. Lemons

Q. What is the smallest breed of dog?
A. The Chihuahua

Fun Fact: The crossbreed of a Chihuahua and Yorkshire Terrier is known as the Chorkie.

Q. Who lives in a pineapple under the sea?
A. SpongeBob SquarePants

Trivia Questions & Answers

Q. Are worker bees male or female?
A. Female

Q. A portrait is a picture of what?
A. A person

Fun Fact: When you make a picture of yourself: it is a self-portrait.

Q. How big is the diameter of a basketball hoop?
A.18 inches

Trivia Questions & Answers

Q. Is the sun a planet or a star?
A. Star

Q. What is the hardest substance in your body?
A. Tooth enamel

Fun Fact: A child has 20 teeth, and an adult has 32.

Q. How many Pups are there in Paw Petrol?
A. 6

Trivia Questions & Answers

Q. What is the color of a school bus?
A. Yellow

Q. What is the hardest natural substance on Earth?
A. Diamond

Fun Fact: Only a diamond can cut another diamond.

Q. When do leaves die?
A. In the fall

Trivia Questions & Answers

Q. How many continents are there?
A. 7

Q. What is the Earth's largest ocean?
A. The Pacific

Fun Fact: The water at the bottom of the Pacific is almost freezing. It's between 34 to 39 degrees Fahrenheit.

Q. Which character slept for 100 years?
A. Sleeping Beauty

Trivia Questions & Answers

Q. Where is the Statue of Liberty located?
A. New York

Q. What team sport is known as the fastest game on Earth?
A. Ice hockey

Fun Fact: The first hockey puck was made of cow dung.

Q. What are Harry Potter's parents names?
A. James & Lilly

Trivia Questions & Answers

Q. How many inches are in a foot?
A. 12

Q. How many wheels does a tricycle have?
A. Three

Fun Fact: The first pedal-powered tricycle was built in 1789.

Q. How many zeros are in a million?
A. Six

Trivia Questions & Answers

Q. What bird lives in Antarctica and cannot fly?
A. Penguin

Q. How many colors are there in a rainbow?
A. Seven

Fun Fact: The colors, in order from the top, are red, orange, yellow, green, blue, indigo, violet.

Q. Where does Santa Claus live?
A. The North Pole

Trivia Questions & Answers

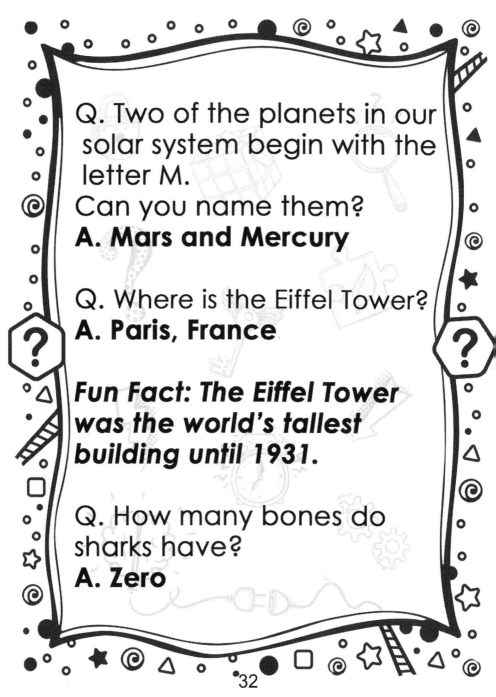

Q. Two of the planets in our solar system begin with the letter M.
Can you name them?
A. Mars and Mercury

Q. Where is the Eiffel Tower?
A. Paris, France

Fun Fact: The Eiffel Tower was the world's tallest building until 1931.

Q. How many bones do sharks have?
A. Zero

Trivia Questions & Answers

Q. The Statue of Liberty came from which country to the United States?
A. France

Q. Where was Christopher Columbus born?
A. Genoa, Italy

Fun Fact: Christopher Columbus made four trips to the Americas, but he only set foot on the mainland on his third journey.

Q. Who was the 16th president of the United States?
A. Abraham Lincoln

Trivia Questions & Answers

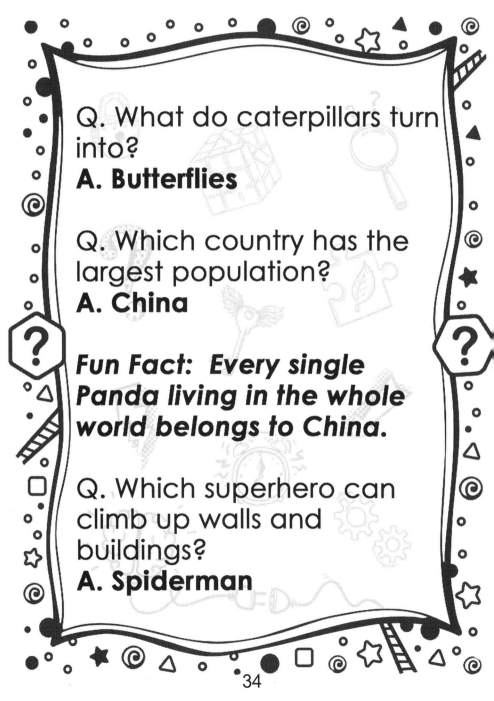

Q. What do caterpillars turn into?
A. Butterflies

Q. Which country has the largest population?
A. China

Fun Fact: Every single Panda living in the whole world belongs to China.

Q. Which superhero can climb up walls and buildings?
A. Spiderman

Trivia Questions & Answers

Q. How many legs does a spider have?
A. 8

Q. What are the primary colors?
A. Red, blue and yellow

Fun Fact: White is not really a color, it is the absence of color.

Q. Who is Peter Pan's main enemy?
A. Captain Hook

Trivia Questions & Answers

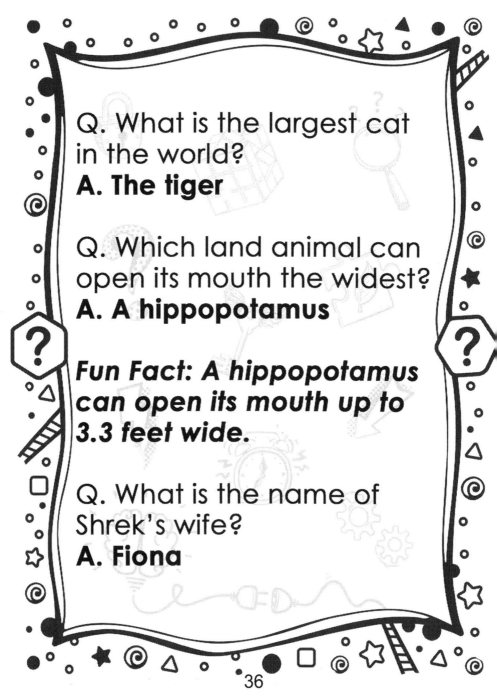

Q. What is the largest cat in the world?
A. The tiger

Q. Which land animal can open its mouth the widest?
A. A hippopotamus

Fun Fact: A hippopotamus can open its mouth up to 3.3 feet wide.

Q. What is the name of Shrek's wife?
A. Fiona

Trivia Questions & Answers

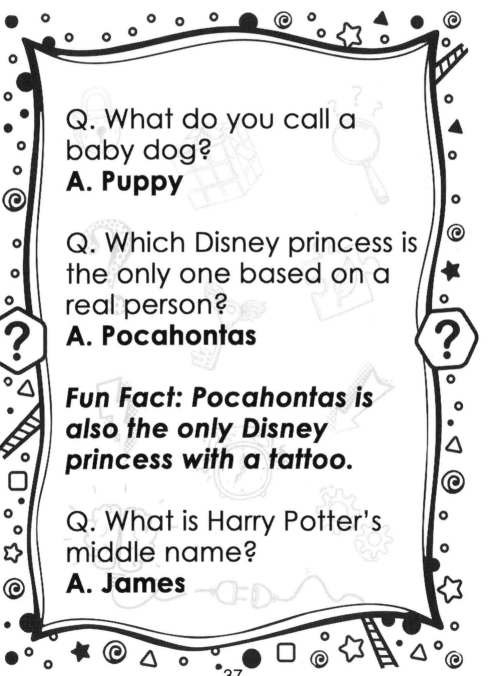

Q. What do you call a baby dog?
A. Puppy

Q. Which Disney princess is the only one based on a real person?
A. Pocahontas

Fun Fact: Pocahontas is also the only Disney princess with a tattoo.

Q. What is Harry Potter's middle name?
A. James

Trivia Questions & Answers

Q. What is a black mamba?
A. Snake

Q. How many "Wonders of the World" are there?
A. Seven

Fun Fact: The Grand Pyramids in Egypt are the only ones still in existence.

Q. Who stole Christmas in a Dr. Seuss story?
A. The Grinch

Trivia Questions & Answers

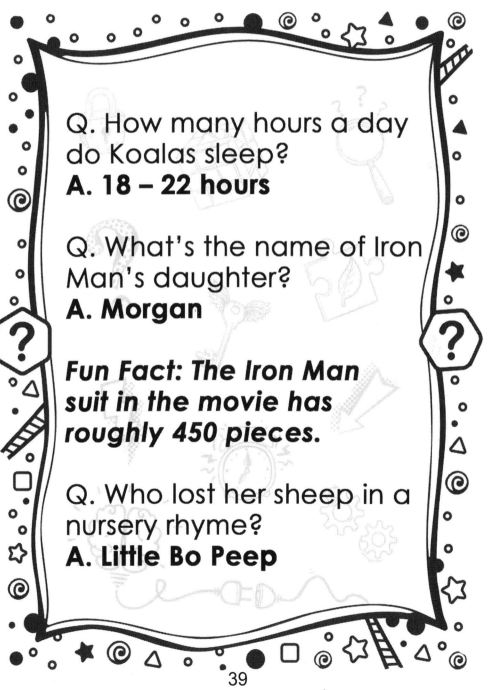

Q. How many hours a day do Koalas sleep?
A. 18 – 22 hours

Q. What's the name of Iron Man's daughter?
A. Morgan

Fun Fact: The Iron Man suit in the movie has roughly 450 pieces.

Q. Who lost her sheep in a nursery rhyme?
A. Little Bo Peep

Trivia Questions & Answers

Q. What is a baby sheep called?
A. Lamb

Q. In Minecraft, what are the smallest mobs in the game?
A. Endermites

Fun Fact: Endermites only have a lifespan of two minutes.

Q. What do you call a baby kangaroo?
A. Joey

Trivia Questions & Answers

Q. What type of animal is the popular TV character, Angelina Ballerina?
A. A mouse

Q. Who invented the telephone?
A. Alexander Graham Bell

Fun Fact: Alexander Bell was born in Scotland.

Q. What is a barracuda?
A. A fish

Trivia Questions & Answers

Q. What is the fastest land animal in the world?
A. Cheetah

Q. Which is the oldest university in the U.S.?
A. Harvard

Fun Fact: Harvard was established in 1636.

Q. Which bird has the largest wing span?
A. Albatross

Trivia Questions & Answers

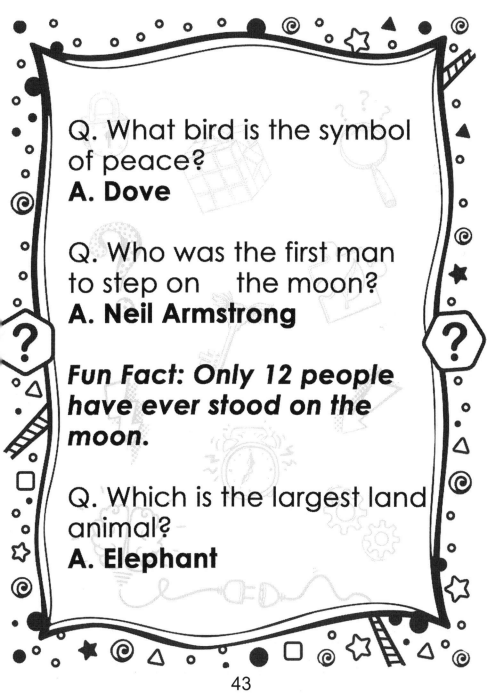

Q. What bird is the symbol of peace?
A. Dove

Q. Who was the first man to step on   the moon?
A. Neil Armstrong

Fun Fact: Only 12 people have ever stood on the moon.

Q. Which is the largest land animal?
A. Elephant

Trivia Questions & Answers

Q. What do tadpoles turn into?
A. Frogs

Q. How many rings are on the Olympic flag?
A. Five

Fun Fact: The first time the rings were used in the Olympics was in 1920.

Q. What could make Harry Potter invisible?
A. The Invisibility Cloak

Trivia Questions & Answers

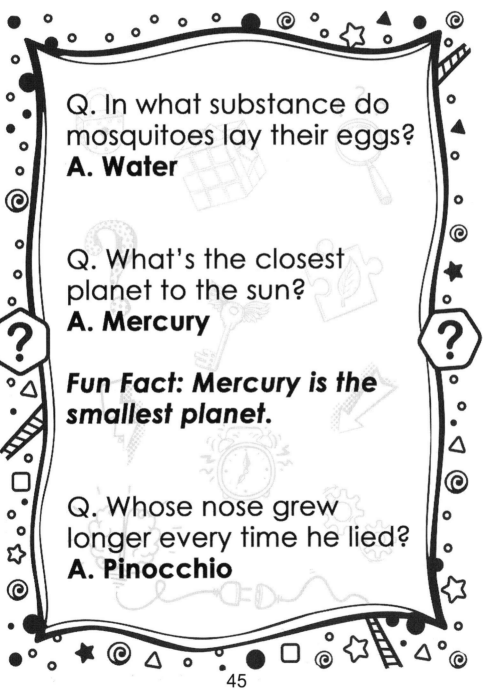

Q. In what substance do mosquitoes lay their eggs?
A. Water

Q. What's the closest planet to the sun?
A. Mercury

Fun Fact: Mercury is the smallest planet.

Q. Whose nose grew longer every time he lied?
A. Pinocchio

Trivia Questions & Answers

Q. Can ostrich fly?
A. No

Q. What was the first animal to be cloned?
A. A sheep

Fun Fact:
She was called Dolly.

Q. What is the name of Anna's sister in Frozen?
A. Elsa

Trivia Questions & Answers

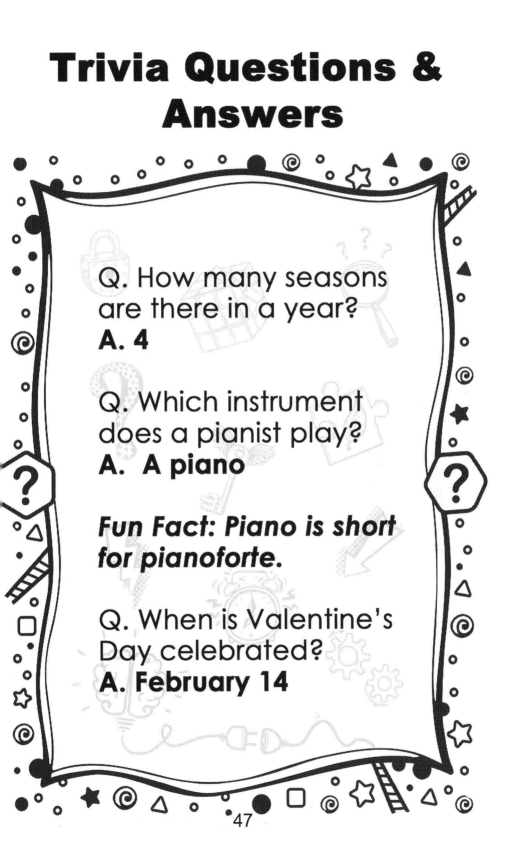

Q. How many seasons are there in a year?
A. 4

Q. Which instrument does a pianist play?
A. A piano

Fun Fact: Piano is short for pianoforte.

Q. When is Valentine's Day celebrated?
A. February 14

What am I?

What am I?

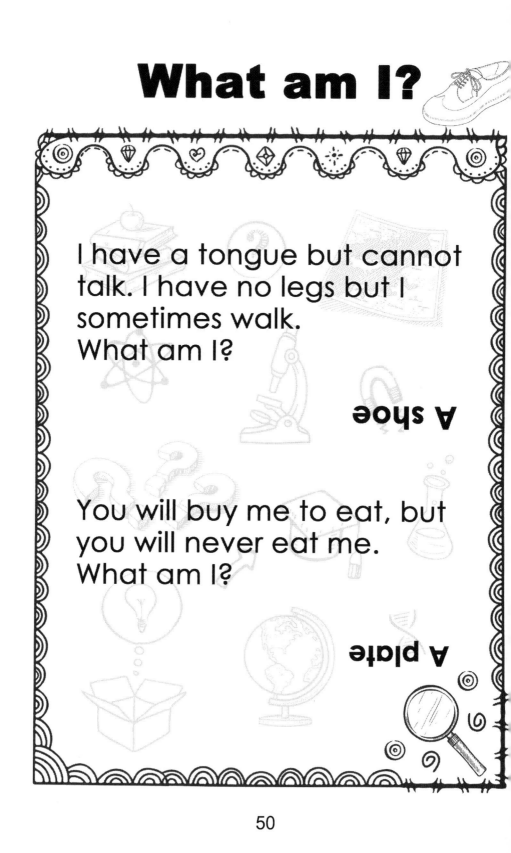

I have a tongue but cannot talk. I have no legs but I sometimes walk.
What am I?

A shoe

You will buy me to eat, but you will never eat me.
What am I?

A plate

What am I?

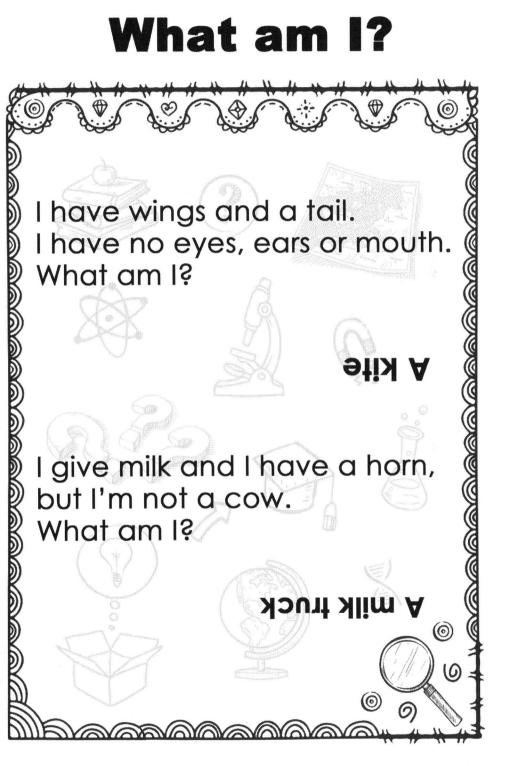

I have wings and a tail.
I have no eyes, ears or mouth.
What am I?

A kite

I give milk and I have a horn,
but I'm not a cow.
What am I?

A milk truck

What am I?

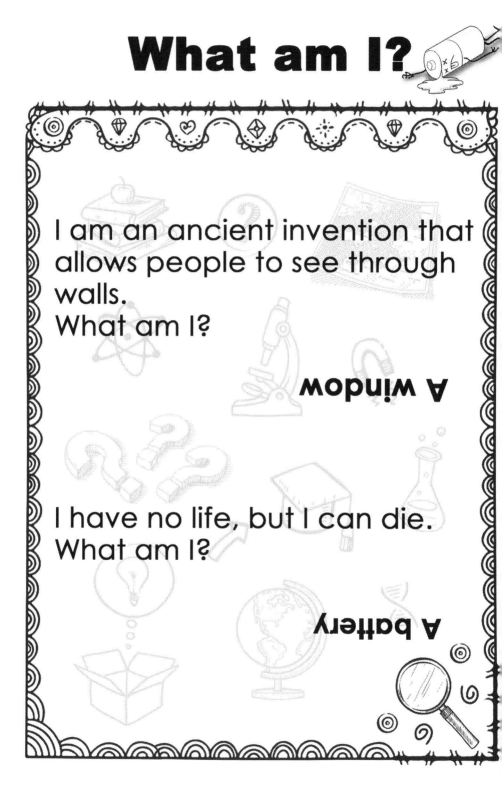

I am an ancient invention that allows people to see through walls.
What am I?

A window

I have no life, but I can die.
What am I?

A battery

What am I?

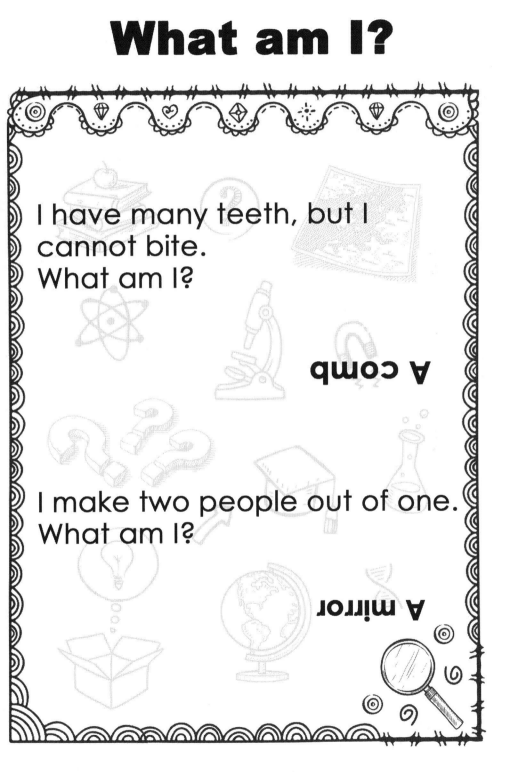

I have many teeth, but I cannot bite.
What am I?

A comb

I make two people out of one.
What am I?

A mirror

What am I?

I have two hands, but I cannot scratch myself.
What am I?

A clock

I have no wings, but I climb to the sky.
What am I?

Smoke

What am I?

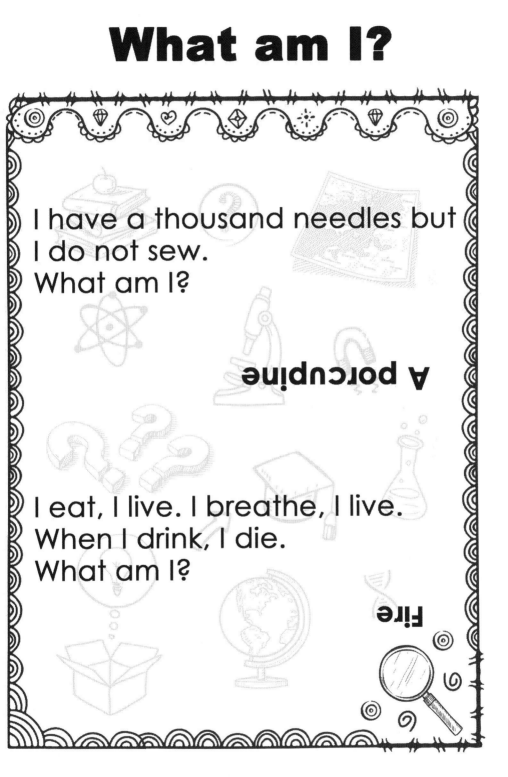

I have a thousand needles but
I do not sew.
What am I?

A porcupine

I eat, I live. I breathe, I live.
When I drink, I die.
What am I?

Fire

What am I?

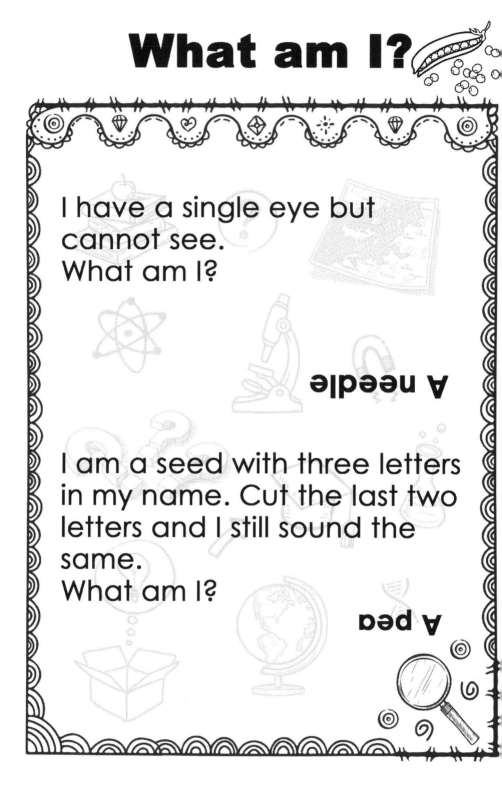

I have a single eye but cannot see.
What am I?

A needle

I am a seed with three letters in my name. Cut the last two letters and I still sound the same.
What am I?

A pea

What am I?

I come down, but I never go up.
What am I?

Rain

I must be broken before you can eat me.
What am I?

An egg

What am I?

I get smaller every time I take a bath.
What am I?

A bar of soap

I have no head, but I have one back and four legs.
What am I?

A bed

What am I?

I disappear every time you say my name.
What am I?

Silence

I can run without legs and fly without wings.
What am I?

Time

What am I?

I have a spine but no bones.
What am I?

A book

I am a very important instrument that you can hear but not touch or see.
What am I?

Your voice

What am I?

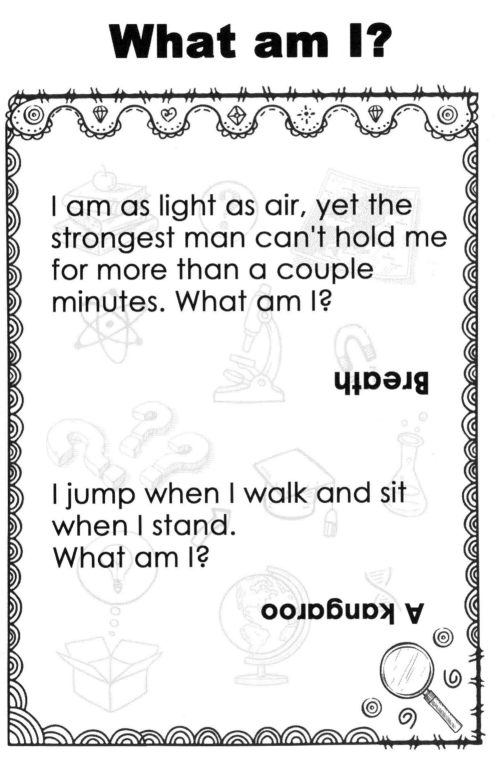

I am as light as air, yet the strongest man can't hold me for more than a couple minutes. What am I?

Breath

I jump when I walk and sit when I stand. What am I?

A kangaroo

What am I?

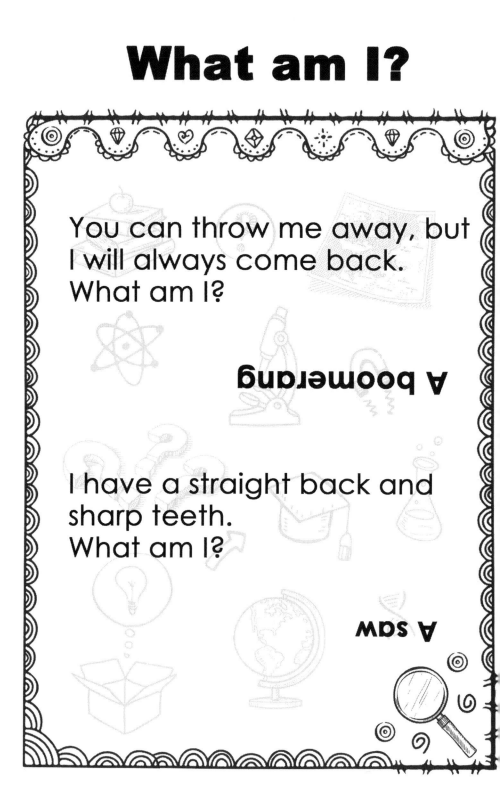

You can throw me away, but I will always come back.
What am I?

A boomerang

I have a straight back and sharp teeth.
What am I?

A saw

What am I?

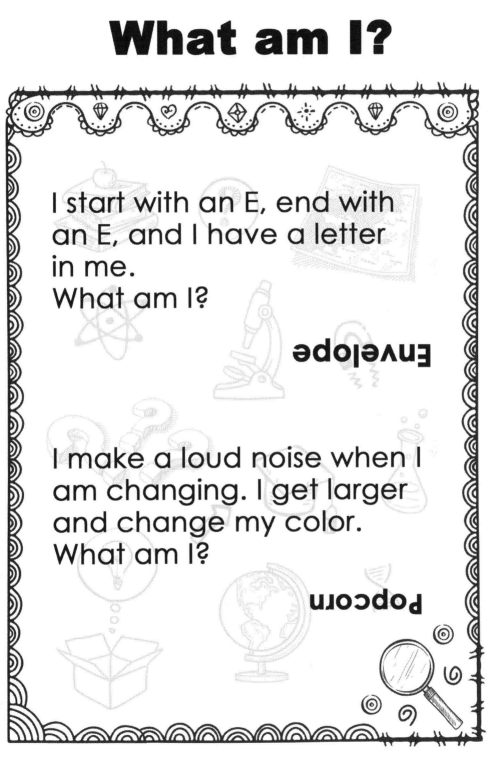

I start with an E, end with an E, and I have a letter in me.
What am I?

Envelope

I make a loud noise when I am changing. I get larger and change my color.
What am I?

Popcorn

What am I?

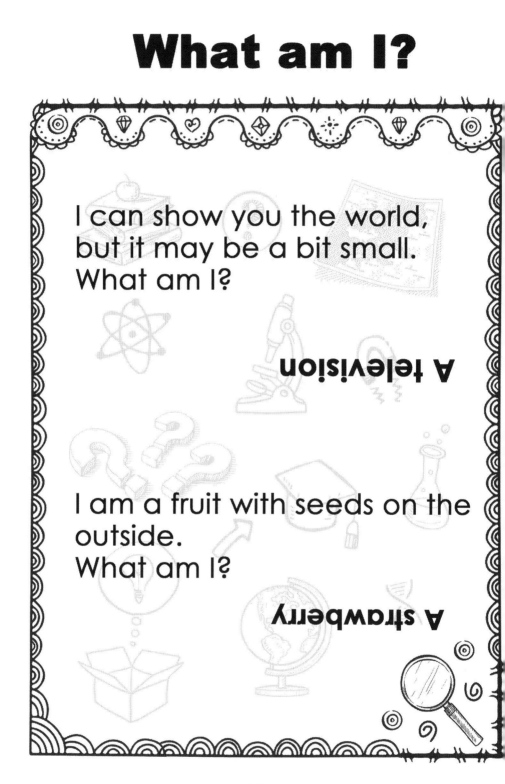

I can show you the world, but it may be a bit small.
What am I?

A television

I am a fruit with seeds on the outside.
What am I?

A strawberry

What am I?

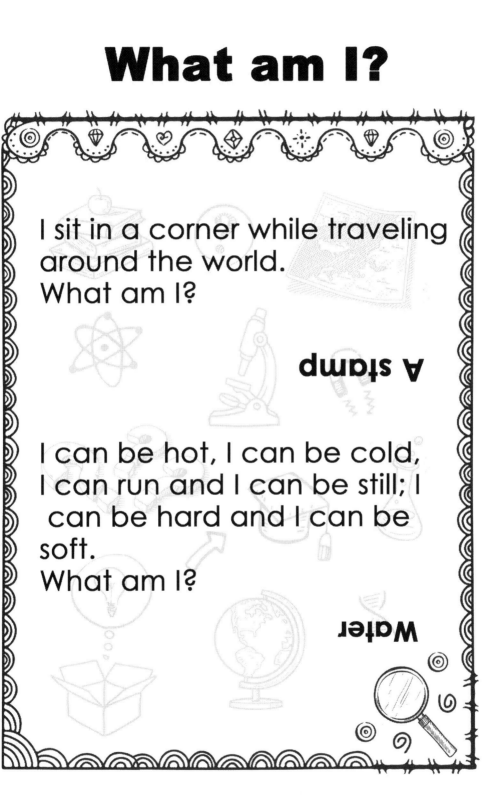

I sit in a corner while traveling around the world.
What am I?

A stamp

I can be hot, I can be cold, I can run and I can be still; I can be hard and I can be soft.
What am I?

Water

What am I?

You find me once in the morning, twice in the afternoon but never in the evening.
What am I?

The letter O

I am white, and as a rule, I scare people.
What am I?

A ghost

What am I?

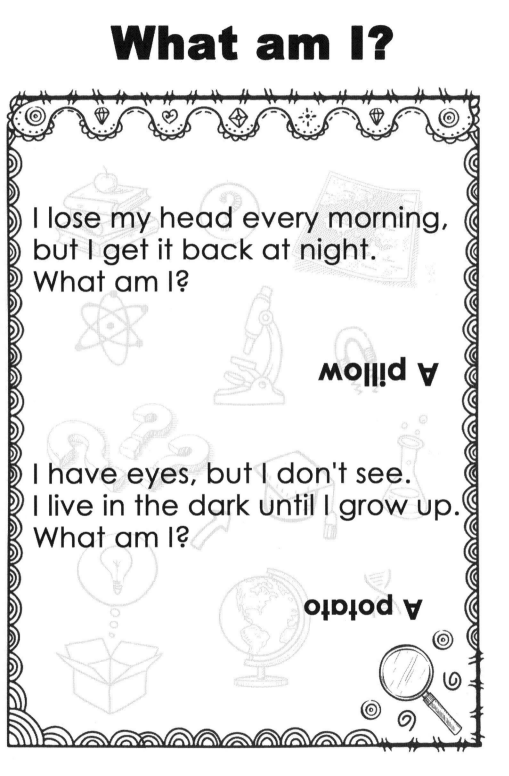

I lose my head every morning,
but I get it back at night.
What am I?

A pillow

I have eyes, but I don't see.
I live in the dark until I grow up.
What am I?

A potato

What am I?

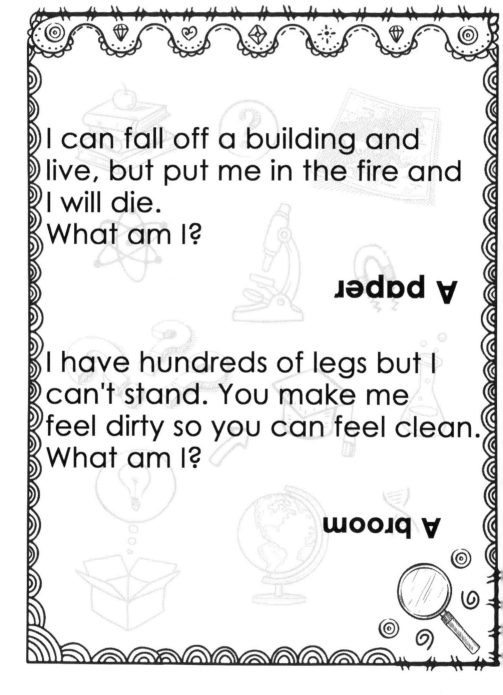

I can fall off a building and live, but put me in the fire and I will die.
What am I?

A paper

I have hundreds of legs but I can't stand. You make me feel dirty so you can feel clean.
What am I?

A broom

What am I?

I can be all colors of the rainbow or have no color at all. Sometimes I'm empty, sometimes I'm full.
What am I?

Glass

I only go up and never come down.
What am I?

Age

What am I?

I am not a holiday. I belong in the month of December, but not in any other month. What am I?

The letter D

The more you take away, the bigger I become. What am I?

A hole

What am I?

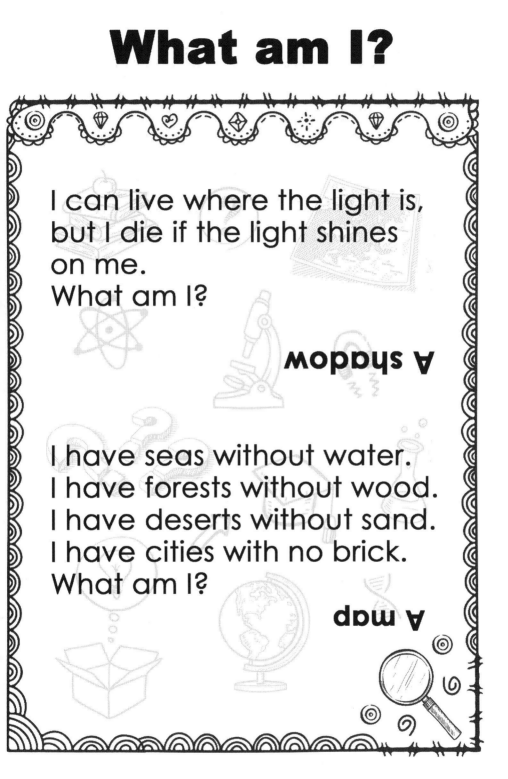

I can live where the light is,
but I die if the light shines
on me.
What am I?

A shadow

I have seas without water.
I have forests without wood.
I have deserts without sand.
I have cities with no brick.
What am I?

A map

What am I?

I sleep when you are awake.
I am awake when you fall
asleep. I can fly but have no
feathers.
What am I?

Bat

People need me, yet they're
always giving me away.
What am I?

Money

What am I?

I am tall when young and
short when I am old.
What am I?

A candle

I am the bloodthirsty beast
you can barely see.
What am I?

A mosquito

What am I?

I go around all the houses, cities, towns and villages, but never come inside.
What am I?

A street

I have a neck, but no head. I have two arms, but no hands. I'm always attached to you.
What am I?

A shirt

What am I?

There are millions of me lighting your way at night.
What am I?

A star *(printed upside down)*

I can connect you to the world but sometimes you ignore me.
What am I?

A cell phone *(printed upside down)*

What am I?

I can bring a smile to your face and a tear to your eye, but I can't be seen.
What am I?

Memories

My rings are not worth much, but they tell my age.
What am I?

A tree

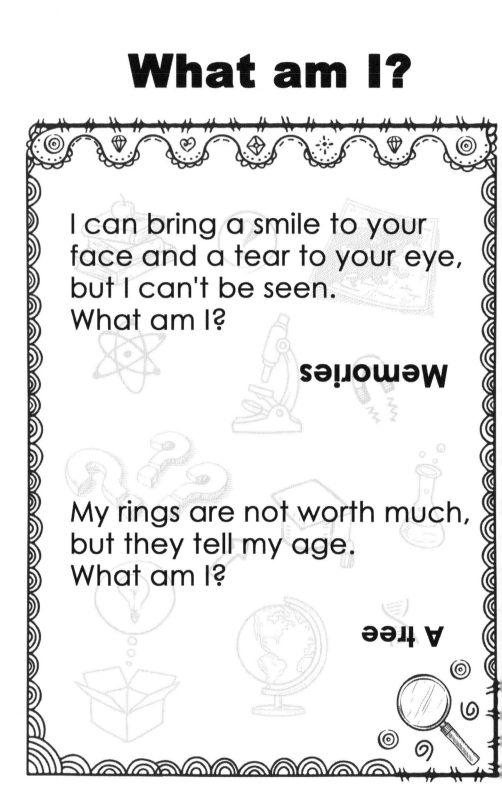

What am I?

I'm always in front of you but cannot be seen.
What am I?

The future

You can catch me but cannot throw me.
What am I?

A cold

What am I?

My best friends make mistakes.
I get rid of them.
Who am I?

An eraser

Born in the ocean. Lived in a small house. Very round I am, and always a lady's delight.
What am I?

A pearl

What am I?

Without me, you would lose your head.
What am I?

A neck

I belong to you, but others use me more often than you do.
What am I?

Your name

What am I?

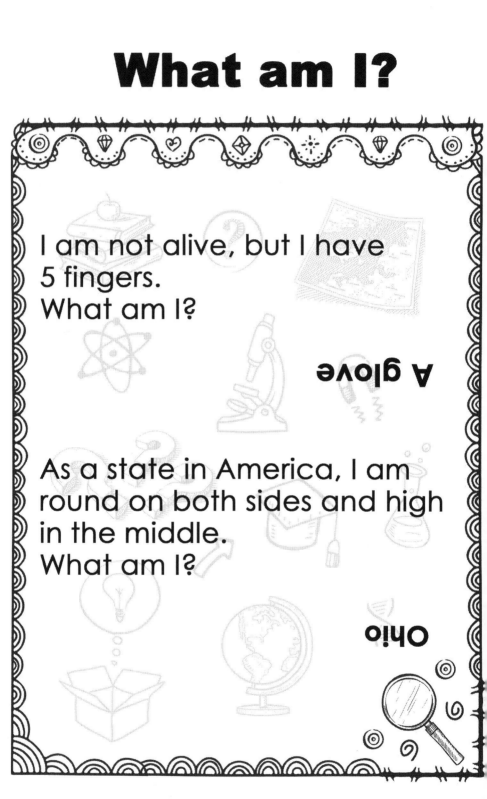

I am not alive, but I have 5 fingers.
What am I?

A glove

As a state in America, I am round on both sides and high in the middle.
What am I?

Ohio

What am I?

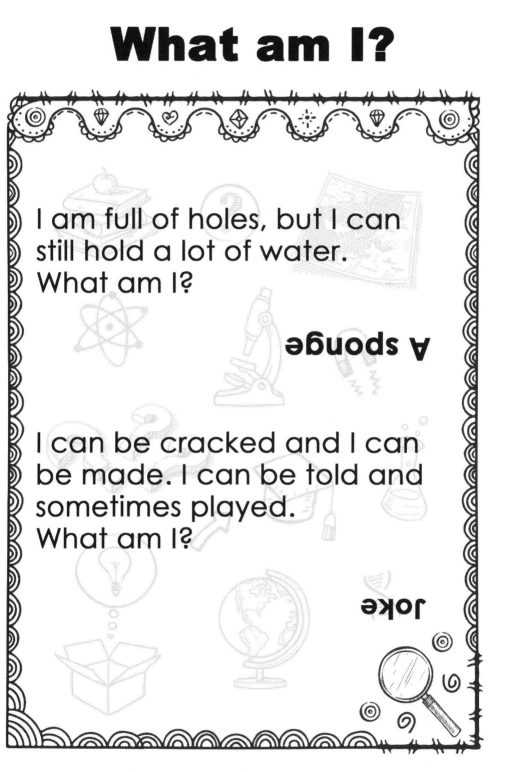

I am full of holes, but I can still hold a lot of water.
What am I?

A sponge

I can be cracked and I can be made. I can be told and sometimes played.
What am I?

Joke

What am I?

I can jump, and I can climb.
With my many legs, I swing
from tree to tree. I can make
a house much bigger than me.
What am I?

A spider

I give people a huge fright,
but at the end, I'm sweet.
I usually celebrate at night.
What am I?

Halloween

What am I?

Better touch me before you proceed to second.
What am I?

First base

I can build or destroy and let creativity soar, but be careful with me at night.
What am I?

Minecraft

What am I?

I can go up and down without moving.
What am I?

The temperature

If you have me, you don't share me. If you share me, you don't have me.
What am I?

A secret

If your kids have enjoyed this book, please consider leaving a short review on the book Amazon page.
It will help others to make an informed decision before buying my book.

Regards,

Robert B. Grand

Made in the USA
Middletown, DE
15 December 2021

56094394R00049